The MAILBOX®

The Education Center®

Caterpillars Butterflies

MW01092094

THE BEST OF The MAILBOX® MAGAZINE

Our best caterpillar and butterfly activities and reproducibles from the 1998–2007 issues of *The Mailbox®* and *Teacher's Helper®* magazines

- **Literacy activities**
- **Learning centers**
- **Group-time activities**
- **Songs, poems, and fingerplays**

- **Math activities**
- **Arts-and-crafts ideas**
- **...and more!**

Fun and practical skills practice!

Managing Editor: Tina Petersen

Editorial Team: Becky S. Andrews, Diane Badden, Kimberley Bruck, Karen A. Brudnak, Pam Crane, Pierce Foster, Tazmen Hansen, Marsha Heim, Lori Z. Henry, Debra Liverman, Kitty Lowrance, Jennifer Nunn, Mark Rainey, Hope Rodgers, Rebecca Saunders, Rachael Traylor, Sharon M. Tresino

www.themailbox.com

Printed in the United States
10 9 8 7 6 5 4 3 2 1

HPS 212076

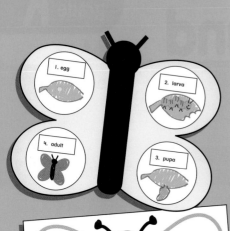

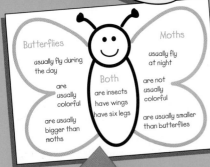

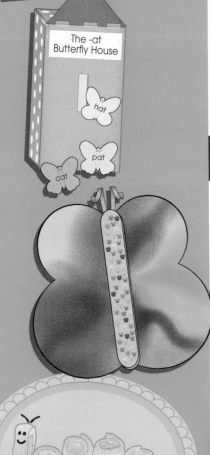

Table of Contents

Thematic Units

Caterpillars & Butterflies • ©The Mailbox® Books • TEC61251

Butterflies!

These colorful ideas are just what you need to brighten literacy, science, and math skills!

ideas by Laurie K. Gibbons
Huntsville, AL

Wonderful Words
Phonological awareness, vocabulary

What's handy about this introduction to butterflies? It doubles as a syllable segmenting activity! Write on the board one of the word pairs shown, writing one word below the other. Read aloud the two words. Then have students clap once for each syllable as they repeat the words. Say and clap the words again to help youngsters determine how many syllables are in each word. Next, guide students to compare how long the words sound and look. After you share the relevant information shown, erase the board and present a different word pair in the same manner. **For more advanced students,** later post the words and a large butterfly to create an eye-catching word bank.

Butterfly Words

- **eggs:** A female butterfly lays eggs.
- **caterpillar:** A caterpillar hatches from an egg.
- **legs:** A butterfly has six legs.
- **insects:** Butterflies are insects.
- **antennae:** A butterfly has two feelers.
- **wings:** Most butterflies have colorful wings.
- **fly:** Unlike moths, most butterflies fly during the day.
- **flowers:** Most butterflies eat nectar from flowers.

Beautiful Book
Describing words

Butterflies are certainly pretty, but what other adjectives can be used to tell about them? Invite students to use a variety of describing words with this class book. In advance, make a class supply of large white butterfly-shaped pages and the prompt shown.

To begin, help students brainstorm a list of words that describe butterflies. Next, give each child a page and have him create a butterfly illustration on the upper portion of it. Help him complete a prompt to tell about his butterfly and then glue it below his artwork. Bind students' completed pages behind a colorful butterfly shape; then glue a butterfly body and two antennae to the front cover. Title the book and decorate the front cover as desired.

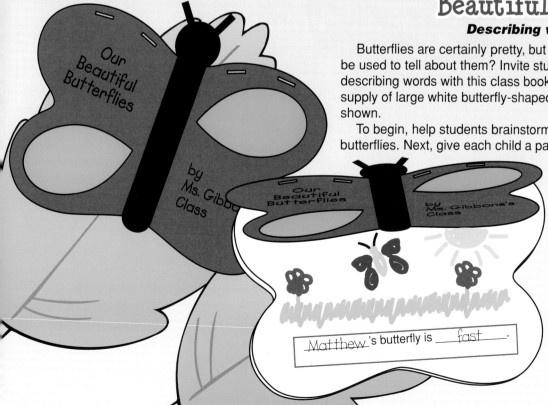

Matthew's butterfly is _____fast_____.

Begin With an Egg!

Life cycle

The wings on this cute project show the transformation from an egg to a butterfly. For each student, trace the butterfly wing pattern on page 6 on a folded piece of construction paper and then cut out the tracing. Each child also needs four white circles, one black butterfly body, black paper scraps, and a set of life cycle labels (patterns and labels on page 6). To begin, read aloud *Waiting for Wings* by Lois Ehlert or *The Very Hungry Caterpillar* by Eric Carle. Review the butterfly life cycle with students. Then use the steps below to help each child make a creative reminder of the four stages.

Steps:

1. Glue the body to the butterfly wings as shown.
2. Cut out the labels. Glue each label at the top of a different circle.
3. Illustrate each circle.
4. Glue the circles on the butterfly's wings in order clockwise, beginning at the top left wing. Draw arrows as shown.
5. Cut two antennae from black paper and then glue them to the butterfly.

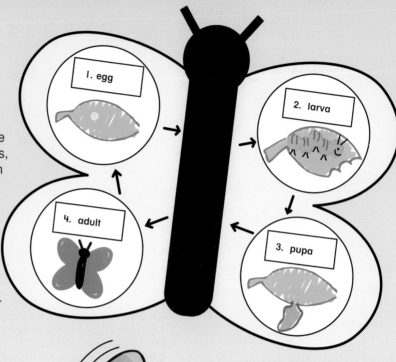

1. egg
2. larva
3. pupa
4. adult

$4 + 6 = 10$

"Pasta-bilities"

Math

What better manipulatives for spring than butterfly pasta? Use food coloring to dye a supply of pasta. (Add a drop or two of rubbing alcohol to the food coloring for more vibrant colors.) Then choose from the center ideas below.

Estimating: Place a supply of pasta in a clear, unbreakable container and label the container with the number of pieces inside. Place different quantities of pasta in two other clear containers. Each student estimates the two quantities, using the labeled container as a guide. Then she writes her estimates on provided paper. After each child completes the activity, help students compare the actual quantities with their estimates.

Measuring: Students use the pasta to measure the lengths of items, such as a pencil, shoelace, and ruler.

Number sentences: Place two colors of pasta in each of several small bags. (Vary the amounts.) For each bag, a student writes a corresponding addition sentence.

Winged Wonders
Symmetry

Your students might be surprised to learn that there is math on the wings of a butterfly! Show students a few photo illustrations of butterflies. Point out that the designs on the wings are symmetrical. Next, give each child a white butterfly cutout. Instruct him to use a black crayon to trace the line of symmetry on his butterfly. Then invite him to color half his butterfly as desired and write his name on the back of it.

After each child completes his coloring, have him trade butterflies with a classmate. Ask him to illustrate the blank half of the butterfly he receives to create symmetrical wings. Display students' completed work on a board titled "High-Flying Symmetry" to remind youngsters that math is everywhere!

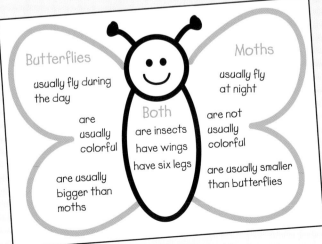

Butterflies

usually fly during the day

are usually colorful

are usually bigger than moths

Both

are insects

have wings

have six legs

Moths

usually fly at night

are not usually colorful

are usually smaller than butterflies

Same but Different
Graphic organizer

Use this adorable version of a Venn diagram to help students compare moths and butterflies or two different butterfly books. Post an enlarged copy of the butterfly pattern on page 7. Title each wing with a chosen topic and label the body "Both." As students brainstorm relevant details, write the information in the appropriate sections. It will be easy for youngsters to see how the topics are alike and different!

Butterfly Patterns and Labels
Use with "Begin With an Egg!" on page 4.

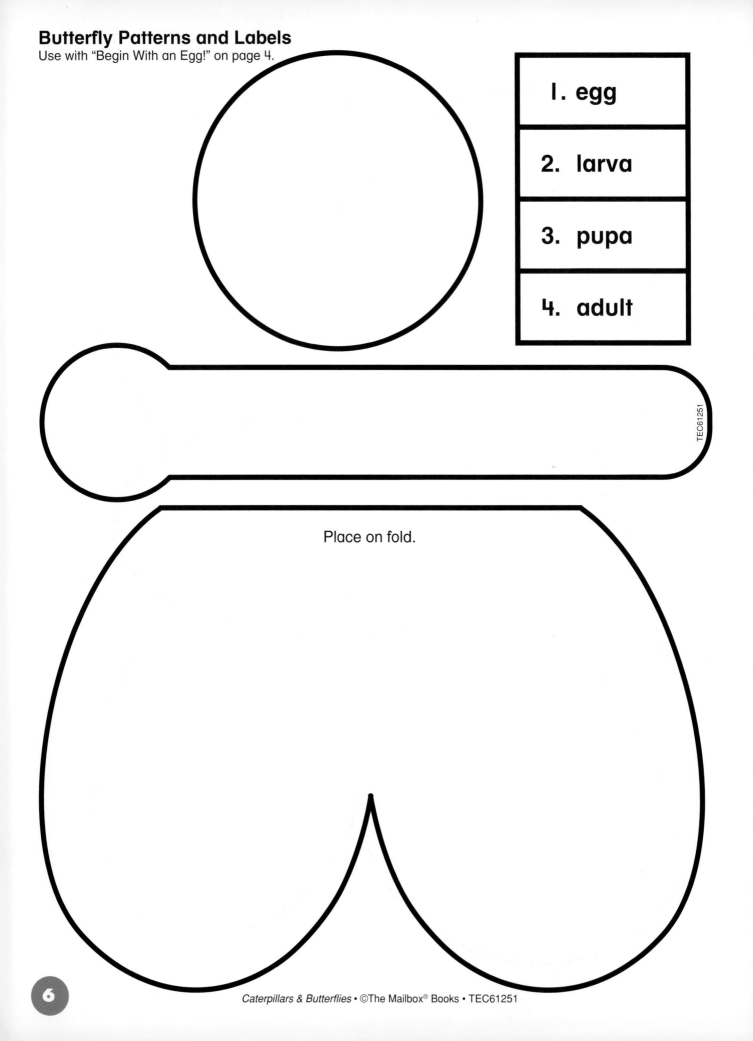

| 1. egg |
| 2. larva |
| 3. pupa |
| 4. adult |

Place on fold.

TEC61251

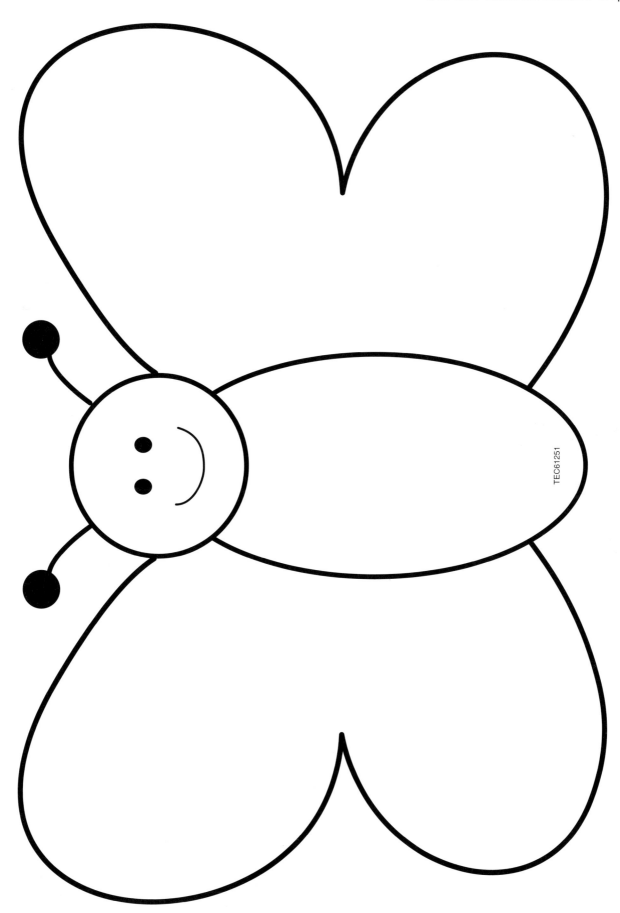

TEC61251

All Aflutter Over Rimes

Your youngsters will take flight while learning about rimes with the ideas in this butterfly-themed unit.

Sorting rimes

Butterfly Houses

Students gain rime-sorting practice when they help little butterflies fly to the right houses! In advance, duplicate the small butterfly patterns on page 10 to make a large supply. Then make a butterfly house for each rime you want students to practice. To make a butterfly house, cover the outside bottom of a shoebox with construction paper. Cut a 1" x 4" rectangle in the bottom of the box as shown. Tape a triangular cardboard roof to the box as shown. Add decorations as desired. Label each house with a different rime. Color and cut out the butterfly patterns. For each house, program several cutouts with words ending with its rime. To make the center self checking, also write the words on the inside of the box. To play, a child sorts the butterflies by rime and then flies them into the appropriate houses. After all the butterflies have been sorted, have him look inside the box to check his work.

The -at Butterfly House

hat

pat

cat

Making words

Building a Butterfly

This butterfly-building activity will have your little ones reading word families! To prepare, make one copy of page 11 for each rime and then color the copies as desired. Label each pattern with a different rime as shown. Program a supply of large craft sticks (butterfly bodies) each with a different consonant. Place the butterflies, the butterfly bodies, paper, and pencils at a center. When a child visits the center, have her choose a butterfly and read its rime. Then instruct her to position a body and read the resulting word. Have her write the words she makes on her paper. Instruct her to circle the real words and underline the nonsense words. Building butterflies—building words!

p et

pet
get
wet
fet
ket
met

8

Attractive Flowers

Little ones will stick to this idea that has them sorting words by rimes. Make three copies of page 10. Color the flower and butterfly patterns as desired. Program each flower with a different rime. Write a different word on each pair of butterflies to match one of the rimes. Slip a paper clip onto each butterfly. Glue a magnet to the back of each flower and then stick them to your board within students' reach. (Use tape if your board is not magnetized.) Draw a stem below each flower. Place the butterflies on the board's tray. Have each child read the word on each butterfly and then place it on the correct flower. What an attractive idea!

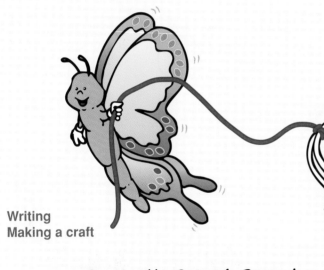

**Writing
Making a craft**

Butterfly Word Families

You'll see lots of fluttering butterflies after youngsters make these word family kites! To prepare, make a class set of page 11. Duplicate the butterflies on page 10 to make a large supply (at least four per child). Cut the butterflies apart. Program each large butterfly pattern with a rime. Give each child a programmed copy of page 11, at least four small butterfly patterns, two three-foot lengths of yarn, and a gift bag. Instruct him to read the rime on his large butterfly and then write one word on each of his small butterflies that includes that rime. Have him color his butterflies as desired and then cut them out. Instruct him to glue his large butterfly to the side of the bag, catching one end of a length of yarn between the bag and the butterfly. Have him tape or glue his small butterflies to the attached yarn length. Then help each child tie his remaining yarn length to the handles as shown. Allow the glue to dry. Then invite each youngster to share his word family butterflies with the class. Finally, take students outside and encourage them to run against the wind to make their butterflies flutter!

Small Butterfly Patterns

Use with "Butterfly Houses" on page 8 and "Attractive Flowers" and "Butterfly Word Families" on page 9.

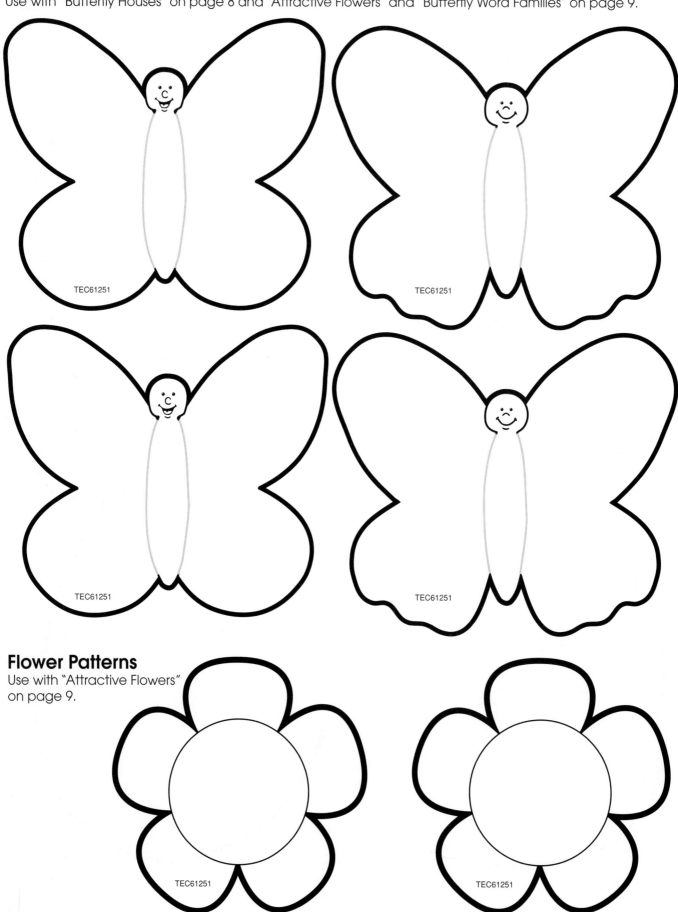

TEC61251

TEC61251

TEC61251

TEC61251

Flower Patterns

Use with "Attractive Flowers" on page 9.

TEC61251

TEC61251

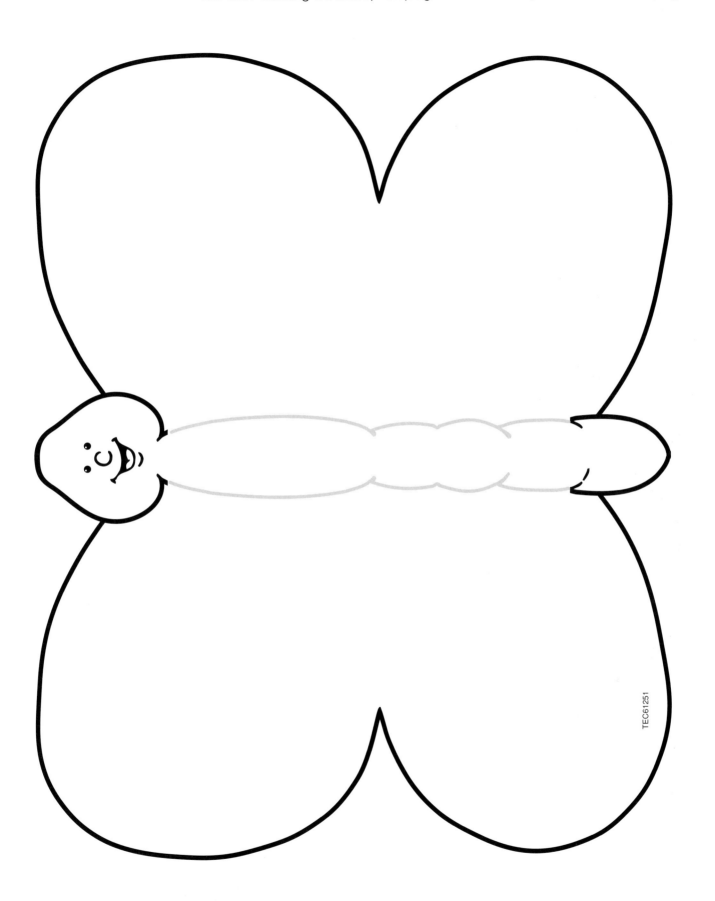

TEC61251

Waiting for Wings

Written and illustrated by Lois Ehlert

The vivid spring garden illustrations and rhyming text of Waiting for Wings will cheerfully teach little ones about the life cycle of a butterfly. Use this book and these activities to help youngsters spread their own creative wings!

ideas by Cindy Daoust

Sequencing
Retelling a story

Sequential Story

Your little butterflies will flutter around this lively sequencing activity! In advance, make a class set of the patterns on page 14. Then cut out a 1½" x 7" construction paper caterpillar for each child. After sharing the book with youngsters, review the butterfly life cycle illustrations. Give each child a caterpillar cutout and a copy of page 14. Have him color and cut out the patterns. Help him sequence the life cycle pictures and then glue them in order onto his caterpillar. Have him color his butterfly and then glue his caterpillar onto it as shown. Have pairs of students take turns using their butterflies to retell the story to each other.

Creating a life cycle model

From Egg to Butterfly

Youngsters are sure to munch their way through this tasty science activity! To prepare, gather a class supply of paper plates, a bag of pretzel twists, and a box of Corn Pops cereal. Discuss with students the butterfly life cycle as you refer to the book illustrations. Guide students to understand that a life cycle is a continuous pattern. Point out that the butterfly life cycle consists of the butterfly egg, the caterpillar, the pupa, and the adult butterfly. Give each child a paper plate, a scoop of cereal (to make the egg, caterpillar, and pupa) and a pretzel (representing the butterfly). Help her arrange and glue cereal and a pretzel onto her plate to create a butterfly life cycle model. Then have her use crayons to draw details on the plate as shown. Finally, let each youngster munch on a fresh scoop of cereal and pretzels.

Butterfly Eggs

Youngsters' rhyming skills will take flight when they help create this "egg-cellent" group game. In advance, gather a basket, a plastic egg for each pair of students, and a class set of three-inch construction paper caterpillar shapes. Give each pair of students one egg and two caterpillars. Ask each pair to think of two rhyming words and then write each word on a separate caterpillar. Check each set of rhyming words. Have each pair put one caterpillar in its egg and then place the egg and the other caterpillar in the basket.

To play the game, ask youngsters to sit in a circle and then pass the basket around for each child to remove an egg or a caterpillar. Ask one child with an egg to crack it open; then help him read the word out loud. Ask each child with a caterpillar to check his word and decide whether it rhymes. Encourage the class to help determine the correct rhyming pair. (Several children may have caterpillars with words with the same rhyme.) Repeat this process until all the rhyming pairs have been matched.

Life cycle
Parts of a butterfly

Flannelboard Flutter

Flitter and flutter to the flannelboard to teach youngsters about the butterfly life cycle. To prepare, gather four 2" pom-poms and cut the following from colored felt: four wings, six legs, one leaf, and one pupa (oval shape large enough to cover a pom-pom caterpillar). Attach the hook side of a Velcro fastener to each pom-pom, creating a butterfly egg and three body parts. Add eyes and yarn antennae to one pom-pom to make a head. Use the flannelboard pieces and the poem shown to illustrate the butterfly life cycle. Then place the flannelboard and pieces at a center and invite each child to have a turn performing the poem.

Look, look—a butterfly egg!
Crawl, crawl on caterpillar legs.
Wait, wait, little pupa.
Soon you'll be a butterfly. Super!

Place the egg on the leaf.
Use three pom-poms to make a caterpillar.
Cover the caterpillar with the pupa.
Remove the pupa; add legs and wings to make a butterfly.

Following directions

Butterfly Garden

Watch your little artists bloom as they create this colorful flower garden that's just waiting for wings. First, make a class set of the construction paper butterfly pattern on page 14. Also gather paints, flower-shaped sponges, and construction paper. Review the beautiful illustrations in the book with youngsters. Encourage each child to use the art materials to make a flower and a leaf. Guide youngsters to use paint to create thumbprint caterpillars on their leaves, and add fingerprints to sponge-painted flowers. Then give each child a butterfly pattern and have him paint one half of it. While the paint is still wet, help him fold the butterfly in half and press down. Then lay it flat to dry. After each child cuts out his creations, arrange them on a bulletin board titled "Our Butterfly Garden."

Life Cycle Pictures
Use with "Sequential Story" on page 12.

Blank Butterfly Pattern
Use with "Sequential Story" on page 12 and "Butterfly Garden" on page 13.

14

More Caterpillar and Butterfly Ideas

C Is for Caterpillar
Beginning sound /c/

These clever caterpillars will have youngsters writing *c*'s and thinking about the /c/ sound. Give each child a sentence strip and have him write uppercase Cs along the length of it. Then direct him to cut out small pictures of items beginning with *c* from a discarded magazine and glue them to his strip as shown. For the final touch, have him draw a face, antennae, and feet on his caterpillar. Cute!

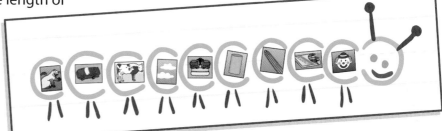

adapted from an idea by Daphne M. Orenshein—Gr. K
Yavneh Hebrew Academy, Los Angeles, CA

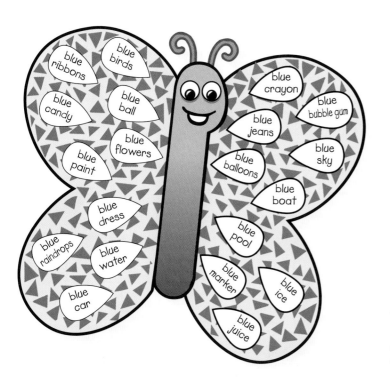

A Colorful Butterfly
Writing

Here's a springtime project that's sure to fly! To prepare, cut out a large butterfly shape from poster board or bulletin board paper. Then choose a color and ask students to brainstorm as many things as they can that are that color. Invite each child to write the name of one of the items in a space on the butterfly's wings. Then have students decorate around the spaces by gluing on crumpled tissue paper of the matching color. Use markers or decorative paper to color the butterfly's body; then add large wiggle eyes and pipe cleaner antennae to complete this colorful creation!

adapted from an idea by Phoebe Sharp—Grs. K and 1
Gillette School, Gillette, NJ

Counting Caterpillar
Counting, identifying colors

Hungry for some math fun? Follow up a reading of Eric Carle's *The Very Hungry Caterpillar* by making these nifty numbered caterpillars! In advance, prepare one caterpillar for each child. To make a caterpillar, cut five six-inch circles from white tagboard. Hole-punch the circles; then tie them together with yarn. Program each caterpillar as shown.

Give each student a caterpillar and guide her to draw the corresponding number of fruit on each circle. Have her color the pieces of fruit appropriately and then add a face to the caterpillar. When the project is complete, use it for counting fun!

Daphne M. Orenshein—Gr. K, Yavneh Hebrew Academy
Los Angeles, CA

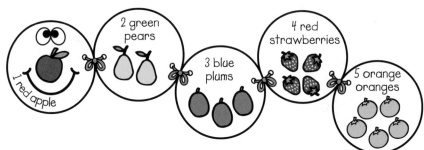

1 red apple
2 green pears
3 blue plums
4 red strawberries
5 orange oranges

I'm So Hungry
Making connections

For a fresh follow-up to Eric Carle's *The Very Hungry Caterpillar*, mount green paper circles on a wall in the shape of a caterpillar; then add a face as shown. Give each child a sheet of copy paper with the sentence starter shown. Have her dictate an ending to the sentence and draw a picture. Mount the papers on the caterpillar background.

Pat Ostrowka—Gr. K, Pilot Elementary, Greensboro, NC

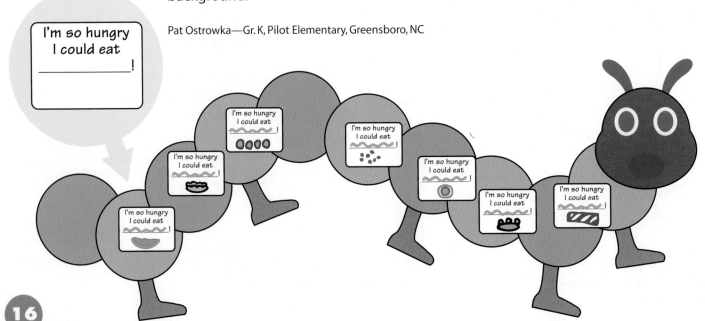

I'm so hungry
I could eat
_____!

I'm a Caterpillar

Written by Jean Marzollo
Illustrated by Judith Moffatt

Munch and crunch your way into simple science with this winsome caterpillar as she takes the reader along on her journey to become a butterfly. After reading the book aloud, review the life cycle of a caterpillar. Then invite each child to create his own caterpillar pin. For each student, provide a tagboard caterpillar cutout (pattern on page 28), four one-inch pom-poms, two paper eyes, black fabric paint, and a pin back. To make a pin, have a child glue the pom-poms on the front of the cutout. Instruct him to use the fabric paint to draw stripes and feet on the pom-poms. After the paint dries, have him glue on the paper eyes; then hot-glue the pin back to the back of the caterpillar. Encourage your students to wear their caterpillar creations at home and share what they've learned about the life cycle of a caterpillar. **Making connections**

Ask me what I will be when I grow up!

Charlie the Caterpillar

Written by Dom DeLuise
Illustrated by Christopher Santoro

Invite student pairs to make a cooperative craft that's sure to remind them of beautiful Charlie! Have each child use clear tape to attach a small picture of herself to one end of a bumpy pipe cleaner. Also have her tape two thin strips of paper to the back side of her photo to resemble antennae. Then explain how each child will turn this caterpillar version of herself into a stunning butterfly with the help of a friend!

Pair students; then give each child a simple butterfly shape cut from a 9" x 12" sheet of construction paper. Have a child choose one color of paint and place a small blob on one of her butterfly's upper wings. Ask her friend to choose another color of paint and dot it on one of the butterfly's lower wings. Have the child fold her paper; then have both children smooth their hands over the wings to spread the paint. Unfold the paper to reveal the butterfly design. Repeat the process with her partner's butterfly shape. Finally, trim each pipe cleaner "body" to the right length and use tacky glue to attach it to the center of the butterfly shape. Display these partner projects with the title "Good Friends Help You Spread Your Wings!" **Making connections**

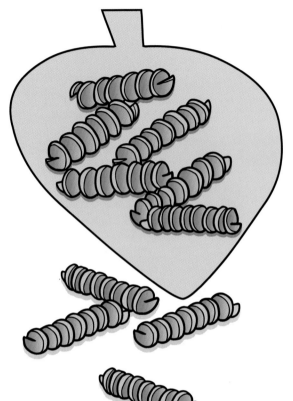

Count on Caterpillars!
Comparing sets

They can creep, and they can crawl, but that's not all. Caterpillars can also help your students compare sets! Give each student a construction paper leaf (pattern on page 29) and ten spiral pasta pieces (caterpillars). Write a number from 1 to 10 on the board; then have each child place that many caterpillars on her leaf. Lead students in counting their caterpillars to check their work. Next, guide students to determine whether they have more caterpillars on or off their leaves. Then ask each youngster to help her caterpillars "crawl" off her leaf to prepare for another number.

Jennifer Stinnett—Gr. K
Arlington Elementary
Arlington, TN

Roll, Add, and Color!
Adding

Students create colorful butterfly pictures as they play this dice game. Divide students into small groups. Give each group crayons, two dice, and a copy of page 30 for each student. To take a turn, a player rolls the dice, announces the sum, and then colors one section on her paper that is labeled with that number. (If there isn't a corresponding section to be colored, her turn is over.) Players take turns until one player wins by coloring all her numbered sections. At the game's conclusion, invite the players with incomplete pictures to finish their coloring before taking their papers home.

Tina Beeler
Lincoln Center Elementary
South St. Paul, MN

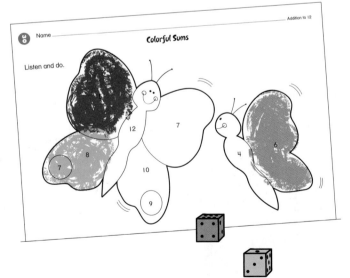

Amazing Changes
Life cycle of a butterfly

Use this "hand-some" project to explore the transformation from caterpillar to butterfly. Set out shallow containers of green, brown, and orange tempera paint. For each child, fold two 6" x 18" construction paper strips in half and then unfold them to make four sections. Staple them together end to end. To make a project, a student cuts apart a copy of one set of the life cycle strips on page 31. He glues them on his construction paper in chronological order as shown. Then he illustrates his paper as indicated. After the paint is dry, he adds desired marker details.

Roxanne LaBell Dearman
Western NC Early Intervention Program for Children Who Are Deaf or Hard of Hearing
Charlotte, NC

> **Illustrations**
> **First section:** Make a row of adjoining green fingerprints with a pinkie finger (small caterpillar).
> **Second section:** Make a row of adjoining green thumbprints (large caterpillar).
> **Third section:** Make a brown paint print with the edge of a fist (chrysalis).
> **Fourth section:** Make two orange handprints as shown (butterfly).

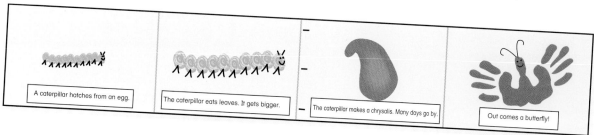

A caterpillar hatches from an egg.

The caterpillar eats leaves. It gets bigger.

The caterpillar makes a chrysalis. Many days go by.

Out comes a butterfly!

Sipping Up Nectar
Investigating living things

This simple activity helps your students understand how a butterfly eats. In advance, gather a small paper cup and straw for each child. Cut a construction paper flower that is two inches larger in diameter than the mouth of the cup; then make two cuts in the center of the flower as shown. Slip a flower onto each cup and tape it in place. Explain to students that most butterflies feed on nectar through a long sucking tube called a *proboscis*. Give each child a straw and a flower cup containing a small amount of juice. Then invite each youngster to use his proboscis (straw) to sip some nectar just like a real butterfly!

Surprise!

Introduce the sign language for *butterfly* (see the illustration). Then encourage children to dramatize the poem with their hands, ending with the butterfly sign.

I am a little caterpillar.
In my cocoon, I go to sleep.
And I won't move about for days.
You won't hear a single peep.
But I know I'll surprise you soon.
And do you know just why?
When the time is right for me,
I'll be a butterfly!

adapted from an idea by Patricia McIntyre—Gr. K
Beechwood on the Bay, Quincy, MA

Traveling Butterflies

Add this delightful song to a study of migrating monarchs.

(sung to the tune of "My Bonnie Lies Over the Ocean")

Verse: A monarch laid eggs on some milkweed,
Then silently fluttered away.
Soon out came a caterpillar
That ate and ate milkweed all day.
Chorus: Monarchs, monarchs,
They are orange and white and black.
Monarchs, monarchs,
We love to see them come back.
Verse: The caterpillar ate lots of milkweed,
Then hung upside down like a *J*.
There soon was a chrysalis hanging
With a pupa hidden away.
Repeat chorus.
Verse: The chrysalis hung there so pretty
For many bright sunny days.
Then out came a pretty butterfly
That silently fluttered away.
Repeat chorus.

Michelle Beckley
Calvin Coolidge Elementary, Binghamton, NY

Class Caterpillar

Looking for a neat end-of-the-year keepsake? Make a T-shirt with this clever caterpillar design that will help students remember their class. To make a shirt, use fabric paint to draw and fill in a cute caterpillar face on the front of the shirt. Then, working with one child at a time, paint the palm and four fingers of one of the child's hands with fabric paint. Have her press the partial handprint onto the shirt. When the paint is dry, write her name on the print with fabric paint or a fabric marker. Continue with student handprints in a line to make the caterpillar's body. Creepy-crawly and cute!

Debbie Musser
Washington-Lee School
Bristol, VA

Winged Wonder

Create a three-dimensional display with several of these butterflies! To prepare, make a copy of the butterfly tracer patterns on page 32. Cut out one pattern along the bold outline. Cut out the inner wing on the other pattern for students to use as a tracer; then discard the rest of that pattern. For each student, fold a 9" x 12" sheet of construction paper in half. Trace the intact butterfly pattern on the fold and then cut out the tracing. Set out colorful tissue paper rectangles and a container of liquid starch thinned with water.

To make one butterfly, trace the inner wing four times on a sheet of white construction paper. Use a paintbrush and the liquid starch mixture to adhere tissue paper to the wings. Let the wings dry for several hours and then cut them out. Next, color the body on the front and back of a folded butterfly. Then unfold the butterfly and glue the inner wings to both sides of it as shown. Glue two narrow strips of black paper to the head to make antennae. Glue the body and head closed to complete the project.

Maureen Glennon
Faller Elementary
Ridgecrest, CA

Brilliant Butterflies

Your youngsters are sure to be all aflutter when they make these sparkly butterflies! To prepare, make a supply of butterfly templates sized to fit on coffee filters (pattern on page 33). To make a butterfly, paint an entire coffee filter with watercolor paints. After the paint is dry, trace a template on the filter. Cut out the tracing. Next, cut two narrow construction paper strips to make antennae. Curl one end of each strip around a pencil and then glue the strips to one end of a craft stick as shown. Glue the craft stick in the center of the butterfly to resemble a body and then glue on colorful sequins to decorate it.

Leanne Gibbons
Boston Public Schools
Mattapan, MA

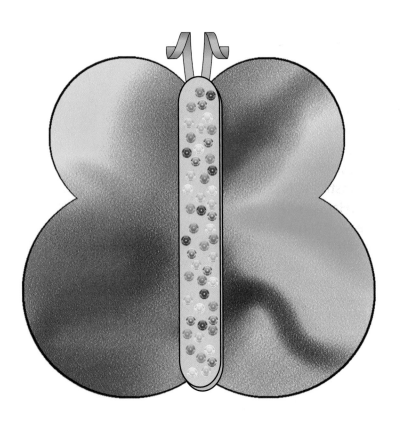

Beautiful Butterflies

Spring into spring with these beautiful butterflies. To prepare, make a class supply of the monarch butterfly pattern on page 34 and then cut each of them out. Stock an area with the following items: butterfly cutouts, a shallow pan of water, spring-type clothespins, and crumpled tissue paper squares in a variety of colors.

To make a butterfly, have each child use a clothespin to hold a piece of tissue paper as shown. Direct him to lightly dip the paper into the water and then press the paper onto a butterfly. The tissue paper's color will bleed onto the butterfly. (Some types of tissue paper will not bleed as much as others. Be sure to test the tissue paper first.) Encourage the child to use this procedure to paint his butterfly a variety of colors. Display these masterpieces in your room or in a hallway and invite visitors to flutter by the butterflies!

Jean Gomes—Special Education, K–2, M. Carey School, Waverly, IA

"Scent-sational" Butterflies

A swarm of pretty-smelling butterflies is about to flutter into your classroom! Copy the butterfly patterns on page 35 on colorful tagboard to make a class set. Give each student a copy of the pattern and have him cut it out. Instruct him to color the butterfly body and draw a face. Have each child apply a generous amount of glue to each wing and then spread it with his finger. Next, have him add pieces of colorful potpourri to each wing. Allow the glue to dry and then hang each butterfly from the ceiling.

Caroline Gartlan—Gr. K
Shanklin Elementary, Burton, SC

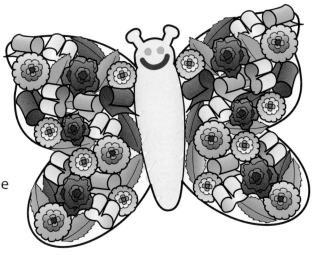

Fancy Wings

Brighten up your classroom with a bounty of these beautiful butterflies.

Materials for one butterfly:
½ of an egg carton (six aligned cups)
tempera paint   hot glue gun
4 coffee filters   paper eyes
water-based markers   pipe cleaners
water
stapler

Directions:
Paint the egg-carton half with tempera paint to resemble a butterfly's body; then let it dry. To decorate the coffee filters (wings), dip the markers into water and then "paint" the filters with the wet markers. (Dried-up markers work for this too!) When the wings are dry, staple each pair of wings together. Next use hot glue to attach them to the body. Add the finishing touches by gluing two eyes and pipe cleaner antennae on one end of the egg carton. Hang these winged beauties from your ceiling.

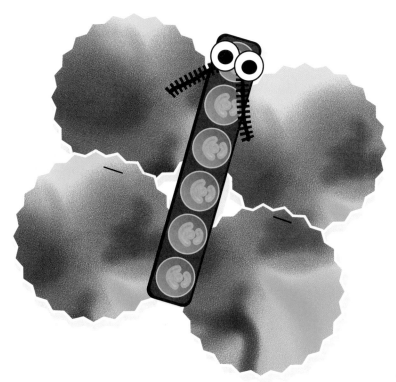

Anita Boomgarden—Gr. K
Chatsworth Elementary
Chatsworth, IL

Sneaking Into Spring

This adaptable board provides each child with her own display space. Cut out a large construction paper circle for each child, plus one extra. Decorate the extra circle to resemble a caterpillar's head. For each child, duplicate a pair of construction paper sneakers (page 36). Have each child color and cut out her sneakers and then glue construction paper legs and sneakers to her personalized caterpillar body part. Mount the body parts behind the caterpillar head, going as far around your room as necessary. Use each body part to display that student's choice of work. (Adapt the title to coincide with your studies—"Sneaking Into Books", "Sneaking Into Science", etc.)

Pamela Buettner—Gr. K, Belleville, IL

This cute caterpillar encourages kindergartners to learn to tie their own shoes! Attach the caterpillar's head to a bulletin board; then add a class supply of paper circles, each labeled with a student's name, for the body. Also cut out a class supply of tiny pairs of shoes (patterns on page 37). As each child learns to tie, have him add a pair of shoes to his caterpillar section.

Lynn Cutshaw—Gr. K, Eastside Elementary, Clewiston, FL

Classroom Café

Caterpillar Roll-Up

Ingredients for one:
slice of bread, crust removed
whipped cream cheese, tinted green
decorating gel

Utensils and supplies:
piece of waxed paper for each student
rolling pin
plastic knives
small disposable plate for each student

Teacher preparation:
- Arrange the supplies and ingredients for easy student access.
- Display a copy of the recipe cards on page 26.

adapted from an idea by Virginia Zeletzki
Banyan Creek Elementary
Delray Beach, FL

Butterfly Snack

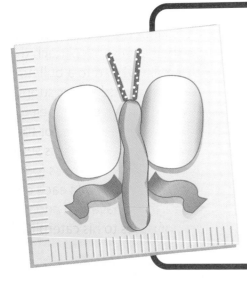

Ingredients for one:
large cheese puff
2 Pringles potato chips
2 Fritos corn chips
2 pretzel sticks
ranch-flavored dip

Supplies:
napkin for each student

Teacher preparation:
- Arrange the supplies and ingredients for easy student access.
- Display a copy of the recipe cards on page 27.

Wendy Arena—Gr. K
Heard-Mixon Elementary School
Covington, GA

Recipe Cards
Use with "Caterpillar Roll-Up" on page 25.

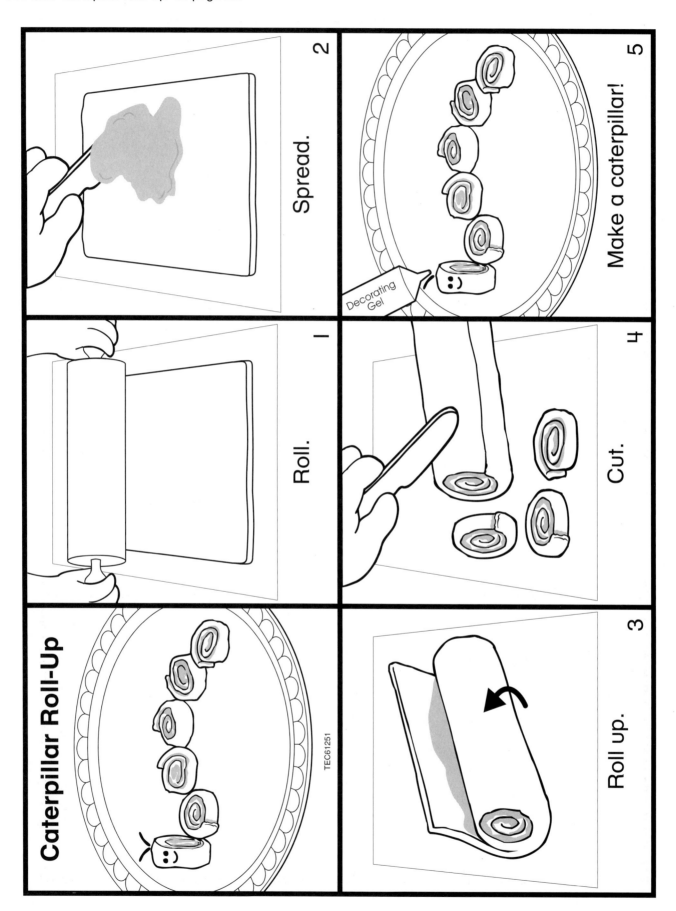

2

Spread.

5

Make a caterpillar!

Decorating Gel

1

Roll.

4

Cut.

Caterpillar Roll-Up

TEC61251

3

Roll up.

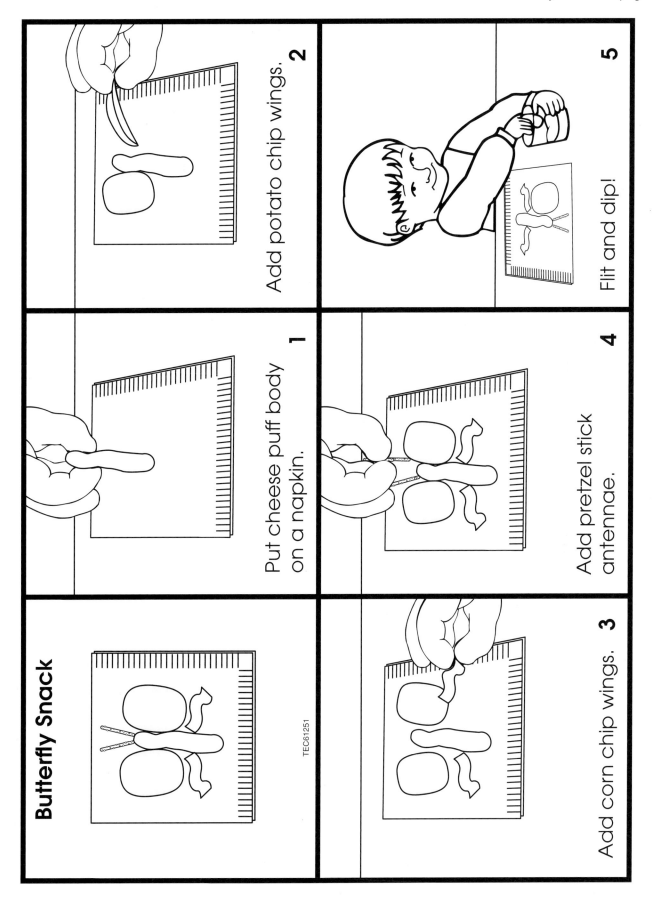

Butterfly Snack

1. Put cheese puff body on a napkin.

2. Add potato chip wings.

3. Add corn chip wings.

4. Add pretzel stick antennae.

5. Flit and dip!

TEC61251

Caterpillar Patterns
Use with *"I'm a Caterpillar"* on page 17.

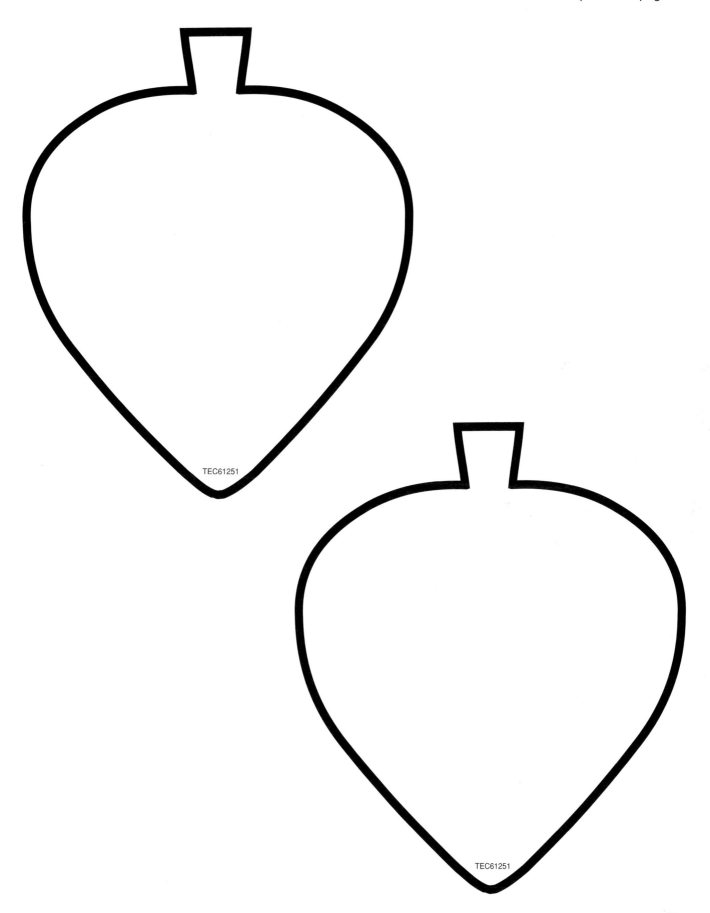

TEC61251

TEC61251

Name _____

Colorful Sums

Listen and do.

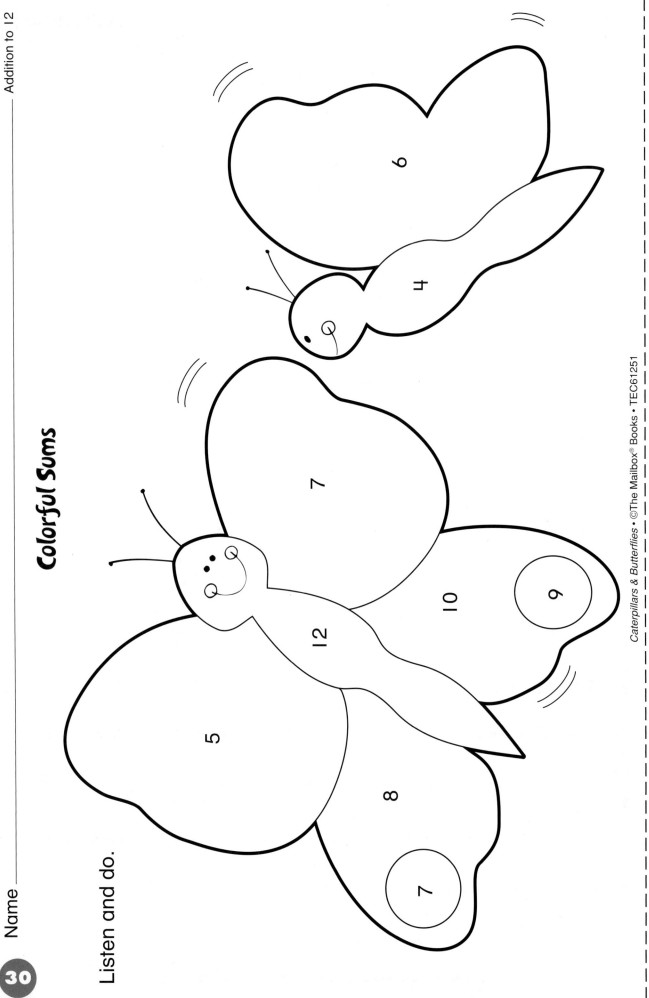

Note to the teacher: Use with "Roll, Add, and Color!" on page 18.

A caterpillar hatches from an egg.

TEC61251

The caterpillar eats leaves. It gets bigger.

The caterpillar makes a chrysalis. Many days go by.

Out comes a butterfly!

A caterpillar hatches from an egg.

TEC61251

The caterpillar eats leaves. It gets bigger.

The caterpillar makes a chrysalis. Many days go by.

Out comes a butterfly!

Butterfly Tracer Patterns
Use with "Winged Wonder" on page 21.

TEC61251

TEC61251

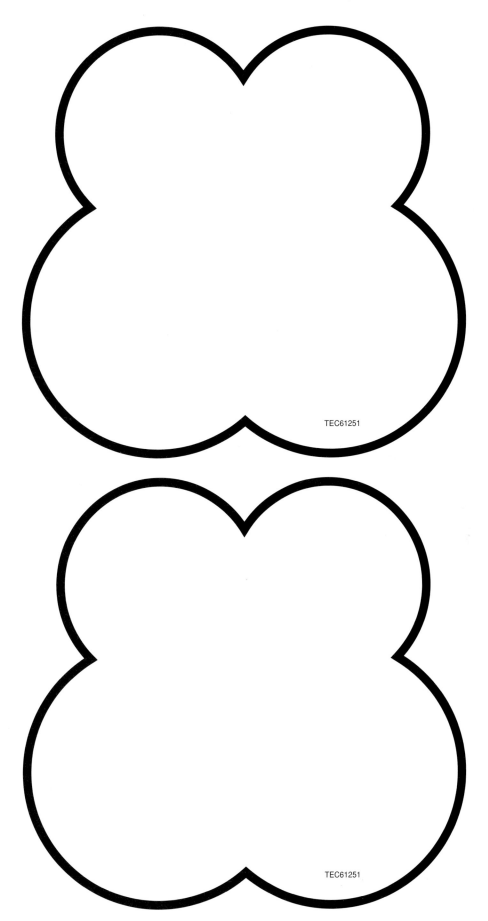

TEC61251

TEC61251

Monarch Butterfly Pattern
Use with "Beautiful Butterflies" on page 22.

TEC61251

TEC61251

Sneaker Patterns
Use with "Sneaking Into Spring" on page 24.

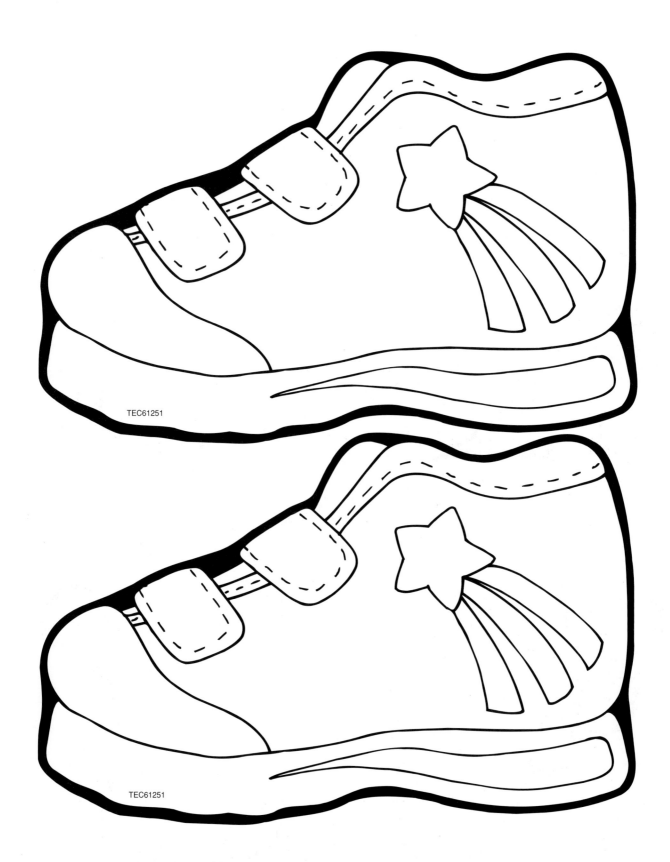

TEC61251

TEC61251

Use with " `Oh my! Look who can tie!" on page 24.

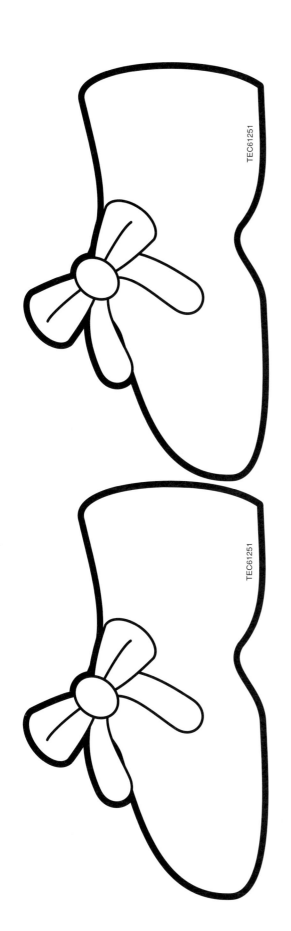

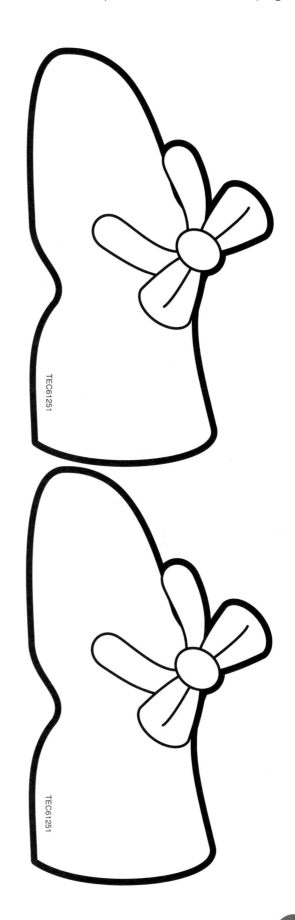

TEC61251

TEC61251

TEC61251

TEC61251

Butterfly Life Cycle Booklet

Materials Needed For Each Student

copy of pages 39–43
crayons
scissors
glue
access to a stapler

How To Use Pages 39–43

Use this booklet to introduce or review the life cycle of a butterfly. Read the text aloud to youngsters and then help them follow the directions below to complete the booklet.

Directions for Each Student

1. Booklet cover: Write your name. Color the butterfly as desired and then cut it out.
2. Booklet pages 1–4: Trace the word. Color and cut out the page and card. Glue the card in the space provided.
3. Sequence the booklet cover and pages, and staple them together along the left side.
4. Read your booklet to a partner.

Finished Sample

Fluttering Butterfly

Butterfly, butterfly,
Fluttering in the breeze,
Tell me about your life,
If you please.

Name _Ashley_

Fluttering Butterfly

Butterfly, butterfly,
Fluttering in the breeze,
Tell me about your life,
If you please.

Name _____

Caterpillars & Butterflies • ©The Mailbox® Books • TEC61251

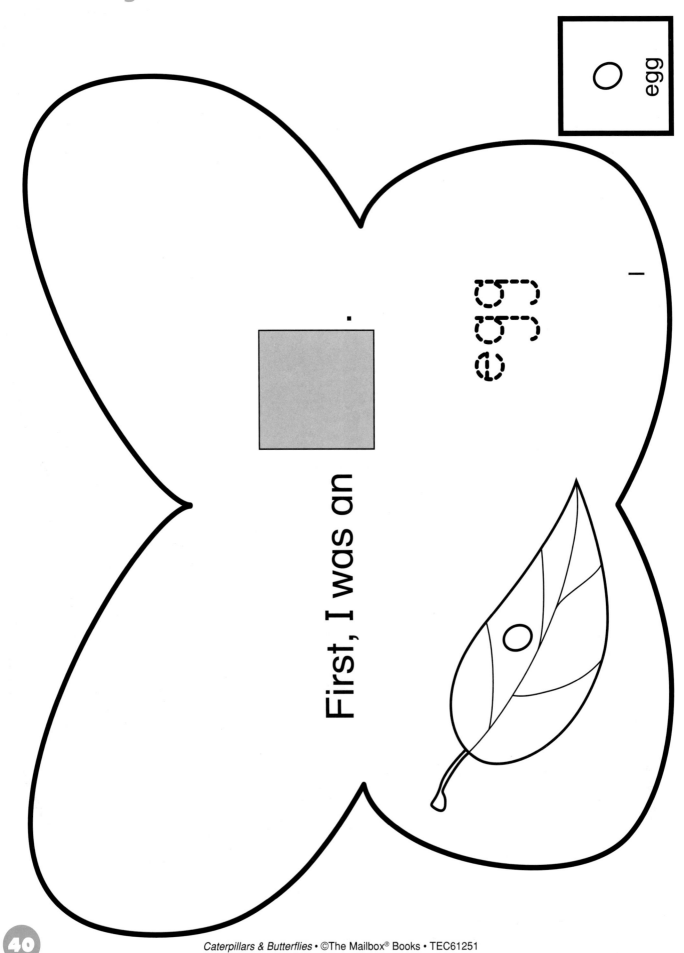

egg

egg

First, I was an

caterpillar

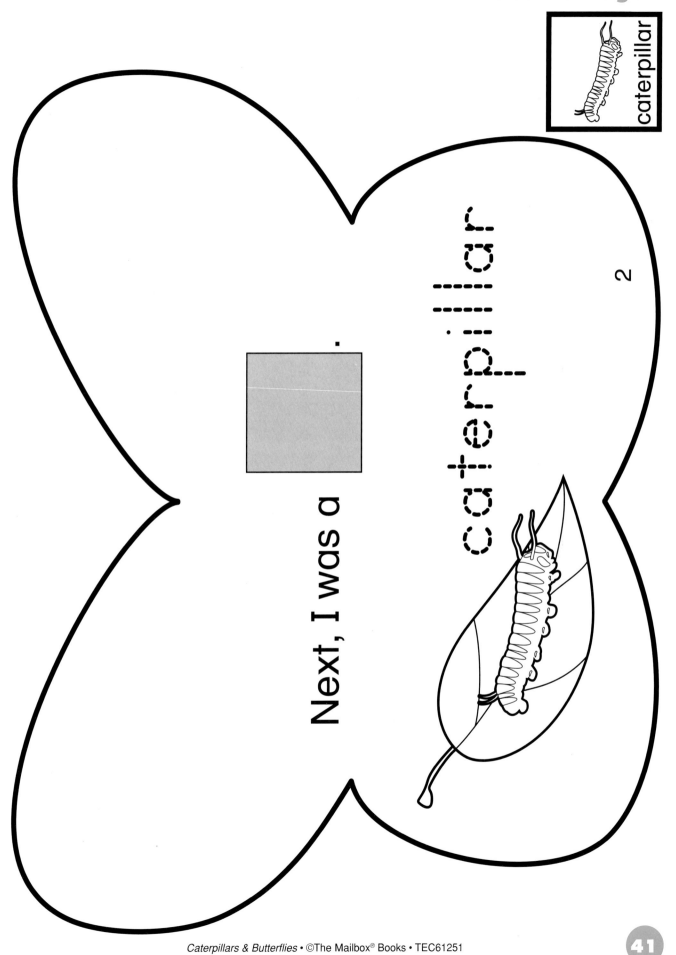

Next, I was a

caterpillar

.

2

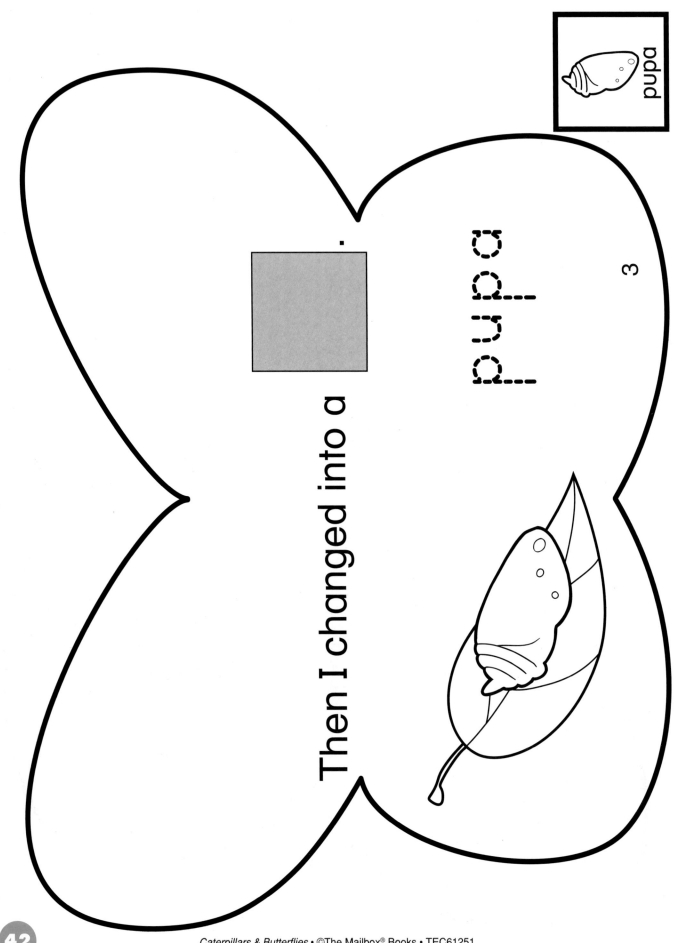

pupa

Then I changed into a

pupa

3

butterfly

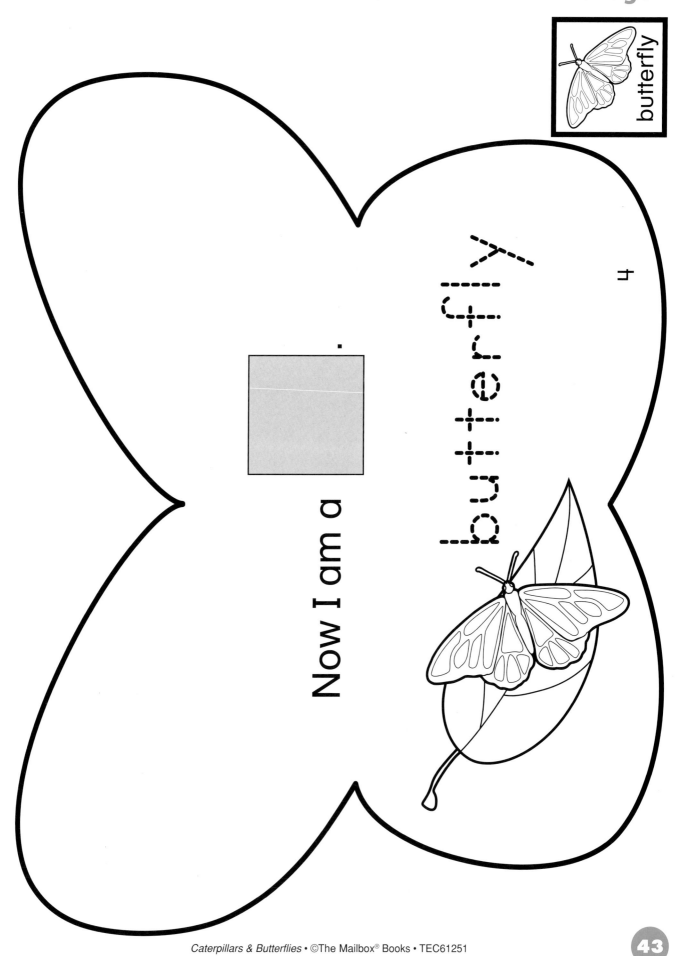

Now I am a ___.

butterfly

4

Prairie Playtime

✏️ Write the ending sound.

Different Butterflies

Count each type.
Color the graph.

Number of Butterflies

Butterfly Type

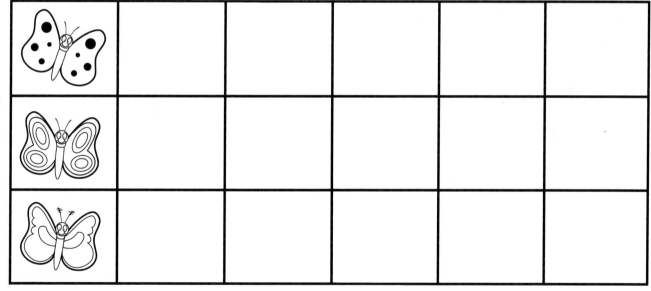

Write.

How many? _____

How many? _____

Circle.

Which has <u>more</u>?

Which has <u>fewer</u>?

Hearts Aflutter

Add.

Write the sum.

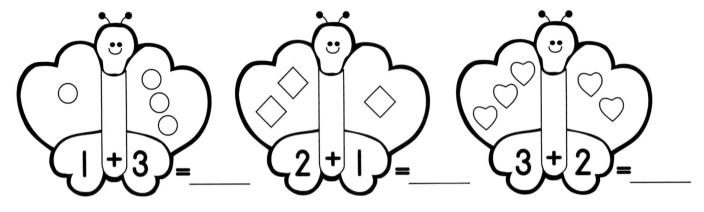

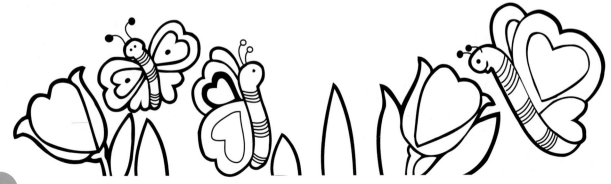

Name

Signs of Spring

Cut.

Glue the spring pictures.

Caterpillars & Butterflies • ©The Mailbox® Books • TEC61251

47

Caterpillars & Butterflies • ©The Mailbox® Books • TEC61251

Note to the teacher: Staple eight sheets of paper between two construction paper covers. Then glue a copy of this page to the front of the resulting journal.